© The Opiate Books 2024
Cover art by: Antonia Alexandra Klimenko
Cover design by: Dale Champlin
ISBN: 978-2-9588567-9-3

# On the Way to Invisible
## (*just passing through*)

selected poems by
Antonia Alexandra Klimenko

*for my son Zack, with love*

# Foreword

On the surface, Antonia Alexandra Klimenko's poems seem to have a certain levity, an undeniable jubilance to them as they dance and delight with their use of language. But it doesn't take too much looking beneath the surface to understand that, as it is said, still waters run deep. Throughout the vivid collection assembled here, AAK manages to encapsulate the wide (and often confusing) range of human emotions, particularly those related to mortality (death, one might even posit, is the ultimate method to achieve being "on the way to invisible"). That unavoidable problem that plagues every human, sooner or later.

Klimenko beautifully describes this phenomenon through the haunting imagery of a poem like "Who's There?," during which she writes, "She stared at me through her windowpane/I looked at her pain through mine/I an aging mime without sound rotting like a frozen vegetable/In the dark in the dark/my icebox is making that awful sound/In the dark my refrigerator is dying." As are all of ours, so to speak, at any given second of the day. And most of what we do is driven by this undercurrent of fear. The fear propelled by the knowledge that, one day, we will no longer be here. Our time will be up, the sand in our proverbial hourglass drained into the wrong side. AAK also subverts death imagery in verses such as the one in "Of Papa Who Sang in the Opera" by illustrating, "Color/of the shit linoleum/I scrubbed with a toothbrush/the day I was forced/to dig my own grave/Punishment for the crimes I committed/like living."

And it is, to many—particularly those in power—a crime when a person chooses to live. Really *live*. As opposed to just existing. Keeping your head down, falling in line, etc. That's all the average Oppressor wants out of those it controls. But poets in general and poets like Klimenko in particular live their lives in direct defiance of what is deemed "the norm" in this life. Which, in effect, is to walk around like a dead person, a zombie. Never questioning and certainly never enjoying. Klimenko, instead, exhibits a bold, rebellious *joie de vivre* throughout this inspiring work. For it's not all death and decay, darlings (though, as AAK points out, "Your only safe alibi is death"). There's also plenty about passion and love, the two things that many have forgotten how to feel in this life of increasing technological coldness.

Hopefully, *On the Way to Invisible* will help you remember how to experience those sentiments again, how to allow them in at the risk of also allowing in the "unpleasant feelings" that can result in the aftermath of the euphoria-inducing ones. The "unpleasant feelings" that have caused many people to switch off their emotions altogether in favor of feeling nothing at all. If anyone can inspire and incite this remembrance, it's Klimenko and her poetry.

Genna Rivieccio
Editor, The Opiate Books
Summer 2024

# Table of Contents

## I

| | |
|---|---|
| The Illusionist | 2 |
| Heritage | 4 |
| Who's There? | 8 |
| Glass Nobodies | 12 |
| Of Papa Who Sang in the Opera | 15 |

## II

| | |
|---|---|
| Metropolis | 18 |
| Interrogation of the Moon | 22 |
| July | 24 |
| The Travel Channel | 26 |
| Let Me Be Honest With You | 27 |

## III

| | |
|---|---|
| Frère Lampier | 32 |
| Paris in the Afterlife | 34 |
| Heart's Compass | 37 |
| Beautiful Lies | 41 |
| Abracadabra | 45 |

## IV

side order ............................................................................. 48
Holding .................................................................................. 50
When You Are On the Menu ............................................. 52
Pajamas ................................................................................. 55
Old Friends .......................................................................... 56

## V

insomnia ............................................................................... 60
When Death Was a Little Boy ............................................ 62
Twilight ................................................................................. 63
That Cat Named Bird ......................................................... 65
chord in d# minor ............................................................... 67

## VI

Off the Wall .......................................................................... 70
untitled .................................................................................. 72
Crossing Borders ................................................................. 75
Glass Slipper ........................................................................ 78
What's Left Unsaid ............................................................. 79

I

**The Illusionist**

I present to you an ordinary mirror—
a poem in which I will attempt
to recreate a memory before your very eyes—
a dangerous disguise
I must warn you now
don't try this at home

I am after all only a reflection of you
The black dye leaking from my brain
is not real
merely the faint imaging of a cheap out-of-date copy machine
wet with promise
The blood leaking from my veins
is not real
merely a secondhand emotion
like the drool from my painted lips
this printer's ink
that will run slip and sink momentarily
onto the computer screen that is my life

But first let me blindfold the mirror
in which I will seem to appear
and disappear
like dry tears that run to the sea—
that old familiar pull
like the pull of the moon
(not the moon itself mind you
just the reflection)
like the face I am about to make
another deception that requires concentration
that requires something I can only imagine

In this next stanza
with just the faint impression of these words
I will attempt to simulate
the illusion of meaning a bold expression

a river of echoes before you
a river of sighhhhhhhhhs
guaranteed to anesthetize
not pain itself mind you
just the reflection

Remember
this is not a real poem
just the inflection
like the tears i paint
with artificial color
from artificial eyes
the artificial flowers
I throw in shallow graves—
a dangerous disguise

I must warn you again
don't try this at home

**Heritage**

Let's put down roots you said —
buy a house have a kid get a car
Let's not lose another year
wandering like gypsies all over creation

(Mind you
this would be the same year
you planted yourself
in another woman's garden —
the same winter
we buried you in the ground)

Let's not I said
combing centuries from my hair
Let's honor what we've already lost

Everything
slipped through my fingers
that year
Nothing
took root in me
only you
six feet under

I pulled my hair out
by its roots
over you —
for every secret
for every lie
for every betrayal —
one by one
I let my hair down
like a ladder
then descended into Hell

I have always gone to great lengths in my life
Never once cut my hair growing up—
It was a part of me
I wore it coiled
as I would the sun
on the crown of my head
I wore it loosely entwined
with the strands of the moon
Deeply braided
in my Russian-Ukrainian heritage
it was a magical antenna
a conduit to energy both radiant and luminous
 I could tell when you were lying—
see things before they happened

And so
I parted and untangled
your deceptions—
the lipstick lies the lullabies
the gardens you had all but fertilized—
the familiar light filtering through
the subterranean tunnels of my mind
Each tip channeling the sun
scratching at the surface of the moon
Each tip a translucent vibration
of the generations before me

I let my hair down like a ladder
and I descended

Everything sacred
is hidden you said
Not true not true—
though you a mathematician
would reduce me further
In your mind
I am still eclipsed
conquered powerless

buried under you
You who like Genghis Khan
ordered his slaves to wear bangs
across their seeing third eye
Below the surface of my skin—
your original sin
your root of all evil
poking fun at me even now

Once unanchored
it floated up to seek my blessing—
the aorta of consciousness
sending out its arteries—
your veins like rivers
spilling into
my rich fertile soil
just waiting for you
to take hold in me
I who let my hair down
and ascended into Heaven

Every Winter
I tear darkness
from my lips
Every Spring
one by one like weeds
my fingers descendants of earth
wither and sigh and sing into flowers

And where are you, now? I ask—
you a mathematician
wandering still in that other country
looking for the square root of one

Roots do not seek out other lands—
but grow where they are planted
multiplying like numbers
like tears like light

unto themselves a solution
Unlike your blind equation
where centuries are lost
roots find their way back
in the dark

## Who's There?

> *Someone I loved once gave me*
> *a box full of darkness.*
> *It took me years to understand*
> *that this, too, was a gift.*
> -Mary Oliver

An orphan at seven
I had to love the questions —
I didn't have any answers

*Knock knock* I'd say
*Knock knock*
Only no one ever let me in
Only no one even asked, "Who's there?"
so they packed me off to that country
where the moon sucks dreams from a rubber nipple
and I stayed there
and I stayed there

When I was eight
they handed me a doll for my birthday
handed me a doll without a cry
Deaf baby death rattle
glass tears for eyes
Mouth as stiff as her skirt
in a cardboard box
taped on all four sides
taped on all four sides
a cardboard box
for a coffin

And still I rocked her
And still I rocked her

Don't step over the line Honey
don't step over the line —

or they'll snap off your head
and they'll melt you down
for all your plastic truth

Outside
the Pope is playing hopscotch with God
Outside
Mexican borders are crossing themselves at night
Outside
the hems of all the confessors are coming undone
by their own undoing

*Forgive me, Father, for I have sinned*

Stay inside your box Honey
stay inside with me
Let them do your thinking for us

She stared at me through her windowpane
I looked at her pain through mine
I an aging mime without sound
rotting like a frozen vegetable
In the dark in the dark
my icebox is making that awful sound
In the dark
my refrigerator is dying

Don't step over the line Honey
don't step over the line —
stay where you will keep forever
wrapped in your cellophane smile
When Death comes to blow out your candles
close your eyes and make a wish
You can open yourself on your birthday
just don't hold your breath!

When I was nine
I crossed over all the boundaries

rocking back and forth
between moon and madness

*La-dee-dah, la-dee-dah*
And so I rocked me
And so I rocked me

In the hospital   that other country
they watched me
they watched me
so I swallowed a handful of miracles
all of them invisible
all of them blind
I floated out of my body
I floated into your mind
just to know how you were feeling
just to know that I was alive
just to have another answer

Cross over cross over
the voice said
(They'll reduce me to rubber
They'll use me for glue)
Cross over cross over
the voice said
There *is* no division
You're just passing through

Every moment
(breathing out breathing in)
I stand at Life's door
knock knock
I stand at Death's
knock on wood
Oh pick one or the other! I say
Just don't leave splinters in everything!

*Forgive me, Father, for we know not*

Every day
the horizon bleeds rainbows
into herself
*La-dee-dah, la-dee-dah*
as my own dreams
recede into the peeling plastic
of a thousand melting sunlamps
and I am dying
I am dying

Every day
I stand at my own door
I ask the same question
I let myself in
"And what have they done with my dolly?" I ask
No one could teach her to cry Honey
no one could teach her to cry
And so I rock me
And so I rock me

## Glass Nobodies

How I drowned
in my mother's tears
alone and un-rocked
is the part of the story I leave out—
how we shivered and swayed
in the shadow of the storm
how hurricanes had nothing on my father!

Shiver and sway
shiver and sway
That's what I did as a child
that and stare through glass

Did I mention
we lived in a house of glass?
glass windows glass ceilings glass walls
How they called it a greenhouse
How I called it a fish tank—
no air no filter seaweed for supper!
and green stuff growing all around!

People would have paid good money
back then
just to stare
through our glass walls
Our Mother
swishing back and forth
in her Miami salmon Beach chiffon

Did I mention
how re-lent-less-ly
sun and rain beat
on the windowpanes
how our father beat
daily on our dear mother—
our mother

Our Lady of the Aquarium
our mother
gasping for air
like a wail out of water

How we
lay weeping in each other's blood
weeping
in each other's blood
with Jesus
wading through our tears
with Mary
      floating
just above us

How Papa crossed himself
and all four corners of the room—
eye-cons in every corner

Imagine my surprise
when at the age of three
I looked into blood-mirrors
and found my own reflection

And where was Mama?
*Maaaa—maaaaa!*
who died alone at sea
*Maaaa—maaaaa!*
who dove
through a sea of glass
Mama
who could see right through us

And "stay away from the mirrors" she'd warn
Ha! Good luck! That's always a caution
when a hurricane's coming at you
one hundred miles per hour
"And stay away from Papa"

Shiver and sway
shiver and sway
Yes stay away from my father
and other unanticipated flying objects

**Of Papa Who Sang in the Opera**

We buried him   in deep November
brown hat brown suit brown shoes
Color
of sorrow of sepia of sienna
of a thousand burnt photographs
fading into their horizons

Color
of the shit linoleum
I scrubbed with a toothbrush
the day I was forced
to dig my own grave
Punishment
for the crimes I committed
like living

A hole much smaller
than the ones in Papa's head
than the ones in our stories
than the hole in my heart

We buried him above ground
one year at a time
lowering him slowly
into forgiveness—
tulips blossoming
into Soviet red wounds
mouth opening
into Stalin's tomb
Arias by Tchaikovsky
in operatic fury   threatening
to swallow us whole

Lowering him slowly
into forgiveness—
Our father His Holiness

who dreamt of Byzantium
clouds fluttering like butterflies
between   claps of thunder
A pinch of late Autumn blown by the wind
God threw in a handful of stars
The sunflowers looked on
bowing their heads

Sometimes deep in sorrow
I lie in his grave
Papa wanders
      barefoot there
like Jesus Christ in Summer
The Devil too
in his black fedora

II

## Metropolis

> *Take me to the city*
> *Train comin' round the bend*
> *Oh train comin' round the bend*
> -The Velvet Underground

They built this Noise
under the quiet multitude of stars
The sun looked on
the moon feigned sleep
angels peeked
through parting clouds
as numbers crashed
(don't look down)
on Wall Street

Concrete gray columns
of average industrials
sentences whole paragraphs
toppled daily
Reputations   in the red
(splattered)
  onto sidewalks
This Noise
this Teeming Mecca
where hucksters hawked dreams
where money still screams
out window's vacant stare
(look up if you dare)
on the honking sideshow below

Day traders
            for night
night for day
the buzzwords   the sting
the swarm of the deal
played out

in human traffic

Worker drones
who know the drill
spin the spin
money is honey
while bittersweet tears
from deeper pockets
*Buddy, can you spare a dime?**
soon run dry from empty sockets

This Hive
of singular sensation
of relentless rhythm
vertical geography
hybrid choreography
Skyscrapers skyrocketing
through invisible portals
New Yorkers Old Yorkers
those electric immortals
in locomotion of perpetual hum
Queen bees busy bees
the bees knees in yellow taxis
buzzzzing
to the beat of a drum

The faceless matter
the multiplying chatter
of up-and-coming billboards
lookatme lookatme lookatme lookatme
bruised notes   guttered smokes
pavement slick with promise

Silent masturbators
in back alleys tattoo parlors
the corridors of your mind
Tokes from used cigarettes
small-town second-hand strangers

On your breath the scent of death
Buddy, can you spare a dime?

From the other side of my page
just now
"Ohhhh Bay-by Baaaa-beeee"
the lonely slant of consonants
the haunting flesh of vowels
the skeletal skyline
of nectar that once was

Regret
lurks in the shadows
where mostly you pay the rent
hum elegies
to collapsed monuments
between your thighs
the crumbling decay
of ink of liquid obsolescence
that urban grind
his own Harlem brew
that rides the rails
the bend of your throat

We live by our instincts
the steel of our teeth
upscale ourselves
in black velvet night
mourn
Summer's giddy breathless care
Lust's
(Is this all there is???)
fading appetite

hum lullabies
for drifters
the veiled moon
the lament of leaves

train tracks
going
no
where

*lyrics from Jay Gorney's 1932 song, "Brother, Can You Spare A Dime?"*

## Interrogation of the Moon

Where've you been?
Where're you going?
What're you doing?
How long?
Who with?
What for?

He prunes back your favorite rosebush
now a miniature bonsai
This should have been your first clue

He plows through you like pulp fiction—
the next chapter is Poland
This should have been your first clue

He cross-examines your dreams—
some of them escape with only third-degree burns
This should have been your first clue

Later
he will probe holes in your stories
(the size of craters)
They all end badly

He will ask impossible questions
"And what have you done with the stars?"
for which you ponder improbable replies
"I had them for breakfast
when my back was turned?"

He will remind you
he is there to remind you
your only safe alibi is death

The first clue is
there is no second clue

I tell him:
a quick strip-search of this poem
and you will find nothing

Even as I speak
I am eating my own words
One by one...
in reverse order—
the rose petals
the stars
the breadcrumbs in the forest

One by one
they explode on my tongue
they dissolve into the darkness
that stumbles into night

Even as I speak
I am erasing every trace
every feature of my landscape
I am changing my name to Daisy
and I am moving to another town

It's useless to question the moon...
better you interrogate the sun

**July**

I like you July!
I like your sunny yellow bright and sticky
step-right-up-tell-ya-what-I'm-gonna-do days.
Your roll-out-the-sidewalk-cotton-candy-popcorn-vendor
hot-dogs-in-the-mustard roll-in-the-hay days of summer

I like you July!
I like your squeaky high-heeled red patent-leather voice
with those ridiculously low-slung trombone hips
that glide into sound

How you had Manhattan trembling!
How the buildings swayed and collapsed at your feet
as broiling avenues dove into the Hudson
And the jazz-hot dreams melted like ice cream cones
dripping from the bent lamppost
that once enshrined you and your throng

I like you July
I like the red and white and blue of you
the North the South
the black and blue of you
and your gum-chewing tis-of-me humanity
with their roll-of-the-drum eyes
with their hot air balloons
that float on endless strings
in the sky

I like you July!
I like your fireworks in the ignorant dark
how you once tried to bribe the stars to shine less brightly
because you couldn't pay your light bill

And most of all I especially like July
the way you leave me cold with your song and dance…
how I will never bother to look for you in a café

or ask you why
you pawned your soul
for a ride
on the Ferris wheel
in June

I love you July!

## The Travel Channel

> *I sing the body electric.*
> -Walt Whitman

It took me forever to learn how to love—
to love full screen with the volume turned up
with the deep-throated arias
with the heart-bleeding flesh
with the entrails leaking
with that profound wound of womanhood
that waits for you like a bruised ripening hunger
that trembles for you like an unhinged moon
that cries for you as you enter me without a sound

How to scream properly is an art
I do it at night alone in our bed
with the lights off with the TV on—
winding rewinding myself like your favorite rerun

Afraid that you will see the old stories in my eyes
Afraid that you will study my veins like roadmaps
that stretch across the sagging accordion of my ribs
into the rolling hills the deep divide of my conscious being.
that you will mistake my matching carry-on luggage
for that cute set of accessories you will carry-off one day
to that land of used dreams without me

In your mind I am merely a reflection of you—
a mirror with a memory that unfolds now in slow motion
only after you've pulled out of the commercial and already
left the station
The voice that—just before you switch the channel—
knows how to love you with its mouth wide open
and screams faster than you can say fast forward:
*I gave you the remote...now I want it back!*

## Let Me Be Honest With You

I'll be honest with you
Alone in a hotel bed
on Christmas Eve
with neon Jesus
playing to one wall
and *Deep Throat*
oozing through the other
I was looking pretty good to myself
I thought about it—
taking you-know-what into my own hands

How often the moon
comes into her own fullness
in the light of unveiling madness
No less
the ecstasy of stars
the trembling of the earth
the heaving of waves
Why not? then
the shiver through our own joy of being

I'll be honest with you
I felt the shiver of being as a child
but it wasn't exactly joy

I was the one
who never said a word
who nodded smiled
then nodded off to sleep
who shook her head
or shook in terror

the one
with silence
blooming on her lips
like a blood clot or a question mark or a tumor

Two more on my breasts
another you-know-where

And pain—that old scab
wouldn't leave me alone
so I picked at it until it healed
then loved it until it bled

And so it did
all over me
all over creation
all over the canvas of my soul
I think I'd like to be an artist I said

So God in Her mercy
planted meaning on my tongue
and my mouth began to water
And so it grew and multiplied
and I came to call it joy

And joy sang and cried and danced on air
and beat its wings of orgasmic light
leaving a trail
of the mysterious of the Invisible
leading home leading to Grace leading to you

I'll be honest with you
All my life I wanted to fly
I was the one
with shoes so blood-red tight
*I'm coming I'm coming*
I'd whisper
into God's ear
as I limped
all the way to Kingdom come

I come to you
in the becoming of me

offering myself
in waves of pleasure
in waves of sorrow
in waves of prayer
hoping it is true this time
this gift of love

Let me be honest with you
we say
bearing our bodies
but not our souls
Wanting to touch
to be touched
we tear at our own wrapping
to get inside the gift

I come to you
in the blossoming of me
says the becoming moon
to the being sun
year after year
again and again
as they come and go in the dark

I am finally coming
into myself J.B.
is what we say
announcing our own arrival
in board meetings
in bored rooms
in strange towns
before
mirrors lovers and other strangers

We offer ourselves
to ourselves
tearing at the wrapping
parting the tissue

seeking the gift
only to find
the box empty
the moment sorely wanting

They say
the joy that isn't shared
is the joy that dies young
I am old now and full of joy
I am young now and filled with sadness

Let me be honest with you
Neither
has ever fallen
in silence from my lips
nor sat waiting for me
under a tree

III

## Frère Lampier

*(for George Whitman, friend and proprietor of Shakespeare & Co.)*
*Now that my ladder is gone*
*I must lie down where all my ladders start*
                                        -Yeats

It begins with a step
And then another And another
Each step making possible
the step that follows
Each step always the first step
Even the uppermost rung so sincere
it is always the last to know

The climb is never the same
but it is always out of oneself—
out of the bloody rag and bruised rubble
of the soul Out of the broken tune
that the heart sings and the bones
that whistle through and in the wind

The ladder gives me something
to hold onto  Gives me something
to steady myself when the carpet
is being pulled out from under
And when I fall or falter…
I just continue on

Of course  the ladder is not for everyone
There are those who will not pass under it
let alone climb further into the sky
Further into the sky are the vagabond clouds
Who have no words   and the neighbor
from whom you once borrowed a cup of light
Further floats above and below
like the dream within the dream
Today I cannot get past
all the many hands I have thrown up into the air

It is all that I can do to wave back
Many times I have gone past myself
without even knowing
without ever asking what that is called
like the tribe in Africa that has
no concept no language no word
for tomorrow for later or next

Next is for those who take the elevator
and crash it into the sky
Next is for those who make the distinction
between up and down
(linens on 3
absolution on 7)
and doors that eventually close

With each first step that I take—
*I am the open book of my mind*
*I am the open church of my heart*
*I am the open road of my soul*\*
like this ladder
with windows opening into other worlds
and angels marking their passage

Often   I have set a place at my table
for the "Unknown God" or the stranger
How many times have I dined with an angel
without ever knowing   This I know
At this very moment
there is one helping to steady my ladder

Often   I wonder about all those books in Heaven
and—when my own sunset has come—
who of all the many angels there
will light the lamp for me

*\*George Whitman echoing the sentiments of Walt Whitman in "Song of Myself"*

**Paris in the Afterlife**

In my dream   I am always in Paris
just as the undergarments of her city
slip slowly from view   Here
the smoke is violet and thick with steam
rising from lovers' partings
on railroad platforms  and under moonlit bridges
To the left and right
her voluptuous pillows—soft and yielding...
straight ahead—her rod-iron cathedrals
pointing where   I do not know

Already my balcony sighs I will wait for you
as I pack up this day   in my invisible suitcase
(an overnight bag)
and set off into the mysterious fog
with only my breathless wonder
to vanish into Memory's landscape
like a train through a tunnel

Dreams
   are always on time
   are so obliging   seductive
   do not question why you leave
   where you are from
invite you
   to cross the frontier
   the dotted line
   of reality and illusion
permit you
   to paint unframed
   what you cannot see

With our feet planted firmly on the sky
we are all Impressionists here
Surrealists  too
making our way into the canvas—a floating island—

the soul of Creation
just waiting to be reborn

With each first brushstroke I take
the dark syllables of night
find their shape and form
translating me into a new language
My consonants   once flat and bone-dry
vibrate now with pink flesh-toned vowels—
sound with new color and meaning
though  they too  will slip from view

With each first breath I take
I am becoming who I am
more of who I wish to be
One moment—a single leaf blessed by the sun
Another—the rain with such small hands
                              rowing to God
Nothing goes so well with Everything   I say
as I squeeze this   too  onto the palette—
a silent scream in surround sound
coming to a *cinémathèque* near you

In my dream
I am always coming to you—
coming becoming overflowing with desire—
my breasts brimming with sweet cream
in buckets of champagne—
the white napkins and handkerchiefs waving
in train stations   on boats of departure
springs of arrival   atop staircase landings
in between sentences
returning home    by way of expectation

What is Paris if not to expect?—
if not to dream of her    to want and wish for
an experience that takes you beyond
the borders of your own imagination—

the landlady   who wore mops on her feet
and skated down the corridor to keep the floors clean
the neighbor   who had his cat stuffed
so he could rest in peace in the storefront window
the lover   who landed in the mental ward of Hôtel de Dieu
who escaped in his pajamas one night in the rain
who was dragged from the entrance of Saint-Julien-le-Pauvre
who stood on the bridge and jumped into the Seine

Every night I bury the dead
and keep the dream alive
In my dream I expect you are always
more than a little mad
In my dream you are beautiful and eternal
like Paris   like the Light
which pours through my skylight just now
which sits waiting on the balcony waiting

In my dream
I am always you waiting for me waiting for you
I am coming   I am coming   I whisper
to all my lovely ghosts
In my dream   you are Paris
and Always

## Heart's Compass

You pass through me
like windows on a train—
freeze-framed in Winter
my shattered Spring
I look for you
in all the compartments
of my heart
groping blindly
at flashes of reflection

(Why did you pull out? I ask
At which stop did you finally exit?)

knowing full well
I have swallowed you
the night before
swallowed you
as I have the sun the moon
and all the dead stars—
light-years of your grief
passing through me now

I the cavity of Paris
compass without a needle—
my arteries stretching like roadmaps
across the universe of my heart

How I let you slip through me
I will never know
why
I sent you
to your own dark eclipse
your delirium of narcotic bliss
engraved on the head of a needle

What is it we hold in our hands
that slips through our fingers—
this human landscape of blood and tears
How do we hold onto heart's needle
this compass of compassion
this shining star
this point of reference—
hold onto light lost in a City of Light
hold onto that one magnet that pulls us
to a place where we belong

One day
we may lose true North
lose our way
lose this moment
lose whole continents
of ourselves
like refugees
with nowhere to turn
like I lost you
you who once took refuge
deep inside of me

I still hold South
between my thighs
still wait for you to move me
like the Earth
like this engine pumping blood
this train pumping iron
like Night and hydrangeas
exploding into the ecstasy
of novas and constellations
tunneling the black hole of me
the deep blossoming throat of me—
you my heart's needle—
a singing meteor
that passes through me as light
that hums in me like Spring—

the one place I cannot get to

I am the cavity of Paris
that lovers once poured into —
my heart a weeping sieve
Milky Ways oozing from
the swirling globes of my eyes and breasts —
the trickling cum of humanity
peeling Time from my lips like a mask

At night alone in my bed
I marry the sacred dark of you
I marry the souls of all your dead planets
all the sweet amnesias of heaven
that live inside my head
I curse myself and heavy-lidded Night
that slumbers through the day
I dragging the moon
like my flesh behind me
while Dark goes on and on
like the bottomless sky
with no ending or beginning

Dark knows we are afraid of it
wants only to be loved
I swallow it
as I do my tears
I kiss it
like I drink in air
I stuff the shame of guilt
back into my horizon
praying that light will find me

I am the cavity of Paris
that lovers once poured into —
my heart a weeping sieve
Deep inside myself
inside the shadows I cannot contain —

statues and monuments to the dead—
a whole city of shimmering possibility
rises as smoke above a skyline of ancient syllables
quivering on the tip of my tongue

The pallbearer of my own dead poems
bereft of words divine direction or
a satin box to lay my aching compass
I drift
alone in the dark
alone with you and the breath of Winter
erased by a night that forgives

## Beautiful Lies

Don't be a stranger!
you said
Just come as you are
if I'm still around
that is
and if you're not
well then
come as you aren't

but come nonetheless
ready to peel paint
and poems off every wall
to bid proper adieu
to this tortured chamber
with its weeping window
with its hardwood soul
with its wounded lilies
still licking salt from their pointy spears

Come join me
you said
for
a last little Nothing
before
we leave
all this
behind

Oh
and
if by chance
you just happen
to pass a loaf of bread
disguised as a sandwich
or a bottle of water
impersonating Merlot

Hmmm Swiss cheese could be nice
Yes Swiss is neutral territory
but without the bullet holes this time
or just some raw flesh
with a charming garnish
you know
bring her along   too
We'll make a night of it—
a fright of it—
*and the rockets' red glare*
*the bombs bursting in air*

Blonde Bombshells
brunettes redheads deadheads
if they're still around that is
(you fired your machine gun laugh)
A real party—
a Socialist Party
with red herrings
and my *pasta al pesto*
Green Party manifesto
(Not to forget onion soup
sniff sniff
I blubbered)

And
we'll stay up late
only to fade
into the sun-controllable light
Up
so we can make Art
and Love
and wordless words
like *ooh là là* and *lah-dee-dah*
And
tell each other
beautiful lies like
we'll meet again

but always in the next life

And if
we should pass one another
 on the edge of the Unknown—
the brink of unbearable being
we'll promise to nod
and look the other way
you said you said
with your one arm missing—
your eyes—two flashing fish
swimming in pools of blood—
to look the other way

And
if by chance
I said
you plunge your salty spear
into the random dictionary of my grief—
this life I live by rumor—
if by chance
I
should shuffling one day
find you

on a blind alley in Paris
in the urinal of Forget
the fountainhead of Remember
or
pissing under
some other melting definition—
a bridge of conjoined parentheses—
the footnote's crucifix of stars

please
pretend you don't know me
that I may recognize you at once
for the stranger that I am

know you
by your ordinary ready-made smile
the one that bleeds offstage
in the unsung cacophony
of your cabaret heart

know you
for your violation of syntax
for your wanton obscurity
looking for a café  noir identity
to call its own

No one not even
our literary movement
nor the crystal unconscious second-hand emotion
of the astral ticking clock
can claim the iconic Nothingness of you
shattering every mirrored reflection
that has gone and come before you
Everybody is Nobody to Somebody
I sighed
(disguised as myself)

so
if by chance
we should meet—
my friend—
in the middle
        of this sentence—
surely a life sentence *sans paroles*—
or between the bloodied wine-stained sheets
on some other crumpled page in time
remember
       please
just
come as you aren't

but come

## Abracadabra

*(for Sergio Lifante)*

I cannot see you
but I know that you are there
like the sweet nostalgia of butterfly wings—
the dust of memory between my fingers

Since you have gone   my friend
all the ashtrays in Paris are full
all the bottles are empty
a thousand crows have flown
from your head into mine
clocks at the Musée d'Orsay
have decided to stand still
and Billie Holiday is beginning to sound
a lot like Leonard Cohen

I cannot see you
but I know that you are there—
Two boats passing between two dreams—
drawing the sky's curtain between night and day
I walk with you surreal along the canal—
the winter moon drinking the river's dark

Since you have gone
since you and I have now both decided
that *everyone* in Paris lives on the sixth floor
I wait for you at the top of my landing
I wait for you in small rooms with big hearts
I wait for you in all the stations of the soul
that have no last metro

I wait for you at stations Saint-Germain and Saint-Michel…
where split in two old friend…
you look at me I look at you…
Your last night in Paris still waves back to mine

*walk me to the corner*
*our steps will always rhyme*\*

Then   you turn the corner
as I turn this page


*\*lyrics from Leonard Cohen's 1967 song, "Hey, That's No Way to Say Goodbye"*

IV

## side order

don't leave my bed on sundays
don't go to church to pray
i leave my back door open
and i'm open every day

you can worship at my altar
just get down on your knees
i'm not the flesh of Mary
but i still aim to please

plastic Jesus on my dashboard
my upholstery wearing thin
they say God is dead
but She's just knockin' back a gin

or whiskey in the parlor
milk and honey on the mind
while the Devil's in your pantry
robbing you blind    'course

your hunger for my pleasure's
bound to keep us satisfied
you can hunt for buried treasure
i'll strike oil between your thighs

or tattoo your broken promises
across my breaking heart
have anything on my menu
or just  order à la carte

come worship at my drive-in
come roll a dream or two
smoke the whole damn joint down
boy  it's your funeral  too

they say God is dead
but   Lord knows   She's just chillin'
when the world has gone to hell
come see me if you're willin'

honey   pass the collection plate
you know love takes its toll
come offer up a sin or two
it's good for the soul

## Holding

> *Dying*
> *Is an art, like everything else.*
> *I do it exceptionally well.*
>          -Sylvia Plath

I'll call you   he says
in his best dial-tone voice
hanging up
on the word   you
My long-distance lover
uses up   all his words
calls me "Sugar"
before entering me

in his little black book
before slipping   into mute—
listens to himself   breathe

Heavy breathing   is an art
Holding   holding   holding
my breath...
is my calling

I do it
with my mind open
and my legs crossed
I do it
until I turn blue
I do it
until my bones
sing phosphorescent
through my flesh

Offline   is another thing
Offline   I stare at his photo
shiver   in the immense stillness

the missing   the letting go—
words rusting on my lips
as I slip   hard candy
into my mouth
and suck the receiver

Tonight
the phone rings and rinnnngs sooooo
I almost mistake it for my heart!
The reception is bad—
not the phone line…but his
I can hear it in his voice—
it's numbing timbre   his unspoken cool
and

I am haunted
by that long   distant   voice
inside me
my little cell   my hell   my prison
the voice of my little girl
that rings that dreaded bell
you should have

You   should   have
waited waited
waited waited
waited waited
waited waited

waited
to exhale

waited
for him to call

waited
for this man
you've never met

**When You Are On the Menu**

It begins with an itch
then another   and another—
those screaming red eruptions
on arms   legs   and unmentionables
(Isn't life a bitch!)
the telltale sign of corruption—
bloodstains on your pillow
the viscous film of wet dream
on your shrinking fitted sheets

Who are they?  these creeps
these mites   small flat parasites   big appetites
that live in dark places   alleyways   hidden spaces
who feed off you  in excess
before they retire to the comfort of your bed
where they enjoy easy access   Yum
while you lay sleeping?

These creeping encasements of excrement
that gorge themselves on pleasure
Nightcrawlers who dig for buried treasure
who can survive several months
without a bloodmeal in increments   and in leisure
But then you were always on the menu

Paris is plagued with bedbugs   red bugs
Menu à la carte   Men you can't get rid of
Some   who once lived in your heart
in between the cracks
who live on their backs   and off your flesh
who live for your sex…
sometimes your Ex!
Bloodsuckers who return nightly

Where do they come from?
these scammers-go-lightly

these addicts   who bug you   who bite you
over and over
Engaging  mites  soundbites
*hi dear  hi dear hi dear*
*can I call you can I call you can I call you*
*now? Now? Now?*
*Can I come? I mean…can I come over?*
Over and over—
pesky pests
who want what they want
who can't take NO for an answer
who   like a fly  buzzing incessantly
Reddy kilowatted
can't hear a word you say
until they are finally swatted

Always
I am dressed to kill
*Kills bugs dead*
I take no prisoners
I will annihilate you in the end
with just one look   (I wrote the book!)

But why must I always start from scratch—
that human itch—handled with kid gloves
the sore that never heals or mends
a love bite   a soundbite   a parasite
Paris site   that all-too-familiar need—
Ahhhh…to be loved to be loved to be loved

Pesty men   like cock—roaches
may outlive us all
they will eat you for lunch
live inside your head
reinvent the dead

But those of us
(if we know what's good for us)

53

will leave our own red mark
that kiss-off
before that fatal crunch
that disappears   into the sting of dark
Love never goes unsaid

## Pajamas

I lived in them
through Winter
through Covid
through you
through all the getting over
in a room with no view

Cotton for lounging
flannel for bed
sweats for sofa yoga
or maybe instead
polished linen for Zoom

Wrinkle-free patterns
stars daisies balloons
anonymous mismatched bottoms

Candlelit trysts inside my head
a pair in black silk for all the dead
those I'll never see on dotcom

I wore the loose garment
that suited me best
alone in my room
I forget the rest

**Old Friends**

Every Spring I unearth them—
those chiffon dresses with butterfly wings
in their unfurling dark kimonos
the old notebooks
in their unmarked graves
the dried geraniums
that survived the winter
the old friend
who didn't

Every Spring
I say hello to things
and people to whom
I once said goodbye
Moving forward
I step backward
into a new pattern
in which I am
with only my eyes
unable to fully open
in which I am
with all my senses
able to blindly trust

Whoever planted the earth
the sun    the stars
the seeds from which all blessings grow
the silver tears of meteors that fall like dew
the spring rain wet with promise—
Who tills these thoughts in my fertile head
knew all too well
you cannot harvest
what you do not sow

What is lost from year to year
glances back on us—

passes through our fragile glass —
their mirror into ours
Passes through
as light  as dust
as Memory's  smoke and shadow

Outside my unframed window
the moon is melting   trembling
as white as snow —
as liquid as these timeless hours
I bow to kiss the sky
my feet are planted on
I blossom in the wisdom
of what   I come to know

V

**insomnia**

that long gray yawn
that stretches you
beyond the pale
of your imagination
beyond the remote
of late-nite date nite
white noise Pink Floyd
God
*I wish you were here*

here
the cold breath of absent lovers
in bus terminals
in hospitals
in insane asylums
in graveyards
evaporates as smoke
or vapored angels
all
have disappeared through windows
beyond your trace—

those who you felt close to
but never really touched
the letter you wrote
but never mailed
to the suicide
whose heart you broke
reaches for your mind
just one last time
one last time
one last time

you roll another day
like a stale cigarette
in the all-nite diner of your soul—

a drunken masquerade on parade
in a dingy motel
just killing time
just killing time
let me entertain you

as death
floats around the room
paces the floor with the ticking clock
curls your blood and voyeurs
in and out of you

in and out of
twisted bedsheets
dressers and drawers
shoes and socks
with two left feet
that know you
no better than strangers

it's the inverted world
where
night is day
and day is night
where
right is left
and wrong is right
in the blue and lonely hours
Mirror stares
at her own glass face

## When Death Was a Little Boy

he spilled blood all over the carpet
and no one forgave him except for God
and all the other Big Shots who have hardwood

Jesus placed a rosary of eyes that never close
around his neck   And in his mouth
the mutilated silence of deaf sparrows
whose broken wings turn like blank pages
against the winds of time

Death has plenty of time
He waits patiently among the bruised lilies
with his long sad shadow shading his face
and constantly looking over his shoulder

He never gets any rest
He has heavy bags under his eyes
which he must drag along on all those trips
he never takes himself

Sometimes you can hear him
rattling around and around.
But no one sees Death coming—
only Life and God
whose rosaries are everywhere

Once Death caught a glimpse
of his own reflection in God's eyes
and all his mirrors shattered.
Then they folded like cracked ice—
tequila on the rocks!
He's still picking up where we left off

Oh Death has plenty of time
only...he could use a little rest—
He looks much worse in person!

# Twilight

His love of open space
left blanks between his words
gaps between his teeth
silences within

All intervals in time —
the measure of height and width
the depth in which all things exist
and move moved in him —
a boundless three dimensional
journeying between the planets and the stars
the flat surfaces of his mind

How he distanced himself
from things and people
invading his terrain —
floor space parking space
objects and events which occurred
in the space which occupied him — the Absolute Space —
was beyond even him

Often he would go to great lengths
extending himself
the rings around his eyes —
sunken in their dark orbits
spinning
in some alternate Universe

Space
is relative to position and direction
he said
but only in the physical realm
The celestial beauty of inner space
is infinite
There is no separation between
sunrise and sunset

shadow and light
the dead and the living

Life belongs to both worlds
and to neither—
rests in the breath
inhabits the mystery
of here
and oh so there

He said   he said
taking one last drag
on his burnt-out cigarette
before he shut the door
behind him

Blew his brains out
in the hallway   he did
Now, go to Hell!
he said

# That Cat Named Bird

*Charlie "Bird" Parker, jazz legend, 1920-1955*

He could have squeezed the living daylights out of Hell
And so he did   And at his very leisure
His euphoric appetite for bright pain and dulled pleasures—
hip-hopping be-bopping jammin' slammin'
pumping iron and ironic in metaphoric basements
where swinging trumpets blow—was legendary
His valves those brass knuckles of brute sound
opened like delicate testicles (ah…the swell of it)
under the pressure of his well-manicured hand
Sometimes out of hand But then that was Birdland

He lived for… Oh, what he'd give for:
whole notes suspended from jazz-stained ceilings
ripping renting warbling squealing   A yardbird
desperate to fill the uncompromising space
His face a black hole where stars exploding
collapsed into fusion replaced  glass windows
shattered like melting mirrors from the Ice Age
Nineteen was a nice age   The kid had class
His Cherokee in B-flat—pure synergy—
(unsurpassed) peeled poems off of every wall
drove a silk fist with a twist through blood knowledge
stripped down to the quick   Once he heard the call…

no one could keep that horn in its cage

Dawn and neon merging together echoed
his interpolations   Muted shades of strobing rhythms—
he was a language of collisions—a free fall
of featherless wings   Icarus caught in the wailing gale
the chromatic scale of stark illusion penetrating confusion
soft callused lips cut from the equinox of tonal
depth and fragile power   The cryptic
and unspoken lodged in his bill—a shuttered

windowsill opening into a symphony an epiphany
a sunflower smiling wide in the ache of his throat
The dark chords of his vocabulary—stuttering nocturnal—
perched now in treetops   pronouncing his return

Melodies rose up through rampant leaves of invention
Green summer ferns potted plants rotted plants
April in Paris Bird Gets the Worm Ornithology (no apologies)
Thirty-four years of unearthly episodic breakups breakdowns
a narcotic intervention gave him pause but no rest
Melodies rose up through visions of greatness
sketches of  Miles Monk and Dizzy
burnt bulbs eclipsing distant strains mixing chaotic
in fresh saxophonic, kaleidoscopic dimension

Pneumonia in half breaths a heartfelt diminuendo
What was he thinking?  This is it maybe
This is the moment this is the tone
this is the one sound I can really bring home
No more hot-lining liner notes for the final crescendo
Play me the sudden death of midnights Baby!
Play me the jazz-beaked Bird that old deaf fool
Play me that one impossible screech of a cosmic sage
Blue on ebony   arpeggio of dreaming

No one could keep that horn in its cage!

And in one hush of morning Destiny brushed
his dry parting lips his unfettered hips
the suicidal longing of his cold wet drool
The wick of his short flame lit an interval higher
in a sky of blazing burnout—his fame gone cool
That formless ghost of his haunting moan—
his feathers clipped   nothing lost   nothing wanting
His music out the window   his notes off the page

no one could keep that bird in his cage!

**chord in d♯ minor**

*(for Françoise Marbleu)*

three days of rain
of pain and painted flesh
the moan of empty rooms
and what is left
but the sheeted furniture
the whistle and shuffle of bones
a broken telephone   my own footsteps

how quickly they appear and disappear
those passing tones   these luminous encounters
the changing unseen floating dreams
neither living or dead   but waking

distant strains of miles and coltrane
the reflection of the moon on passing trains
inarticulate fingers suspended over keys
the creaking eaves that echo all is gone
what's left of me? i'm going home

i drift from myself   to major and minor
the percussion of   the brushing of  leaves
a wind in transition   a slur of expression
i am divine imperfection
the rapture of autumn   the sorrow of fall
i lie in my shadow   not me at all

but the one who lives outside myself
who finishes what i've left undone
who sings for you   and eats thin air
who reaches for nothing   and finds nothing there

VI

## Off the Wall

When I die
I want to be stuffed
stuffed and mounted on the wall
like some poor old deer
who got caught in the headlights

Not just the antlers mind you
but the whole fucking catastrophe—
glass eyes   mop of hair
scars stretching beyond Wyoming

Gutted by the skin of my teeth
like dead animals and birds
I want to be filled with that special fake something—
that makes me look like I'm alive—
the stuffing that dreams are made of

When I die
I want to hang around
collect dust
remind everyone
that even if I am well past
my expiration date
I'm still here

Well   perhaps not in any
meaningful way
but a testament to
my long shelf life
(perhaps a little shelfish of me)
Alas...

How strange
to be so prominently displayed
in my own absence...
able now   to appreciate

the trophy I really was
in anticipation

Keeping alive
the art of keeping the dead alive
takes talent—
one I don't have   as of yet
and a souvenir   that won't keep
until only   after I'm gone
Life's funny that way

## untitled

> *The sky is falling, the sky is falling!*
> -Henny Penny

i'm the one
who's never home
when you knock
and if she is
when you don't
admits no one
black or white
living or dead

henny penny had many heads

i'm the trick i performed
long before i was born
like this poem written backwards
i'm the stunt that defies
i'm the cry to deaf eyes
whose only reply is
ashes ashes

the Lord moves in mysterious ways
and i am falling upwards

i'm the earth that turns
and fells me from its tree
i'm the ocean that slides from my shore
i'm a point as moved as any fixed mark
i'm the eyes of the dead potato
that finds its way back in the dark

i'm the blood i give
but never give up
i'm the wine that flows outside the cup
i'm the truth inside the lie

i'm transparent butterfly
the Lord moves in mysterious ways
so why can't you or i?

i'm the play i'm writing without a plot
the word "forget" that i forgot
the regret that once escaped my lips
the mercy that hangs now round my hips
with the pull of gravity
the real of unreality
the all or nothing the nothing of all
the indelible handwriting on the wall
that hummmms like a ghetto rhapsody

i'm the bum in the park who says less is more
the plexiglass sky of the invisible floor
the one who cries just outside your door

i'm the intimate stranger
whose smile will always hint of you
the Living Poem
the anonymous fingerprints of you
the enemy you befriend
whose soul can transcend you
the goodbye that may begin
but can never really end with you

i'm the saint, i'm the sinner
i'm the fish you ate for dinner
i'm the air growing thinner as i sigh
i breathe the breathless
my death is deathless
i'm the song i sing when i rise

i'm the altar kneeling
the all revealing healing of the human kind
i'm the splinters i'm still peeling
from the cross i drag behind

i'm the mold and the molder
i'm the front-row-center-season-ticket-holder
STEP RIGHT UP, FOLKS!
THE MYSTERY...THE STAR YOU'VE WAITED FOR!
i'm the protégée of the original sin
i AM the light i'm buried in

i'm the moth i'm the flame
i'm the prayers for the insane
i'm everywhere and nowhere
please remember my Name

## Crossing Borders

Every night I make the crossing
Every night I ask myself
Where did I come from?
Where am I going?
My body stretched out before me   like a map—
my heart   a broken compass

I   an ancient voyager
    born of an ocean of love
    in a sea of blood—
am traveling to the other side
of what and where   I do not know

I AM
the road I travel
the vehicle that transports me
the passenger   at ALL the stations
I am
a vessel slipping
into each fluid emotion
a silver bullet
tunneling through
the barren wastelands of my mind
the wilderness of my soul
the ravaged forests of love
the deep vast wreckage of me

How dense
these continents of flesh
where needles and stitches
scars reaching beyond borders
have left their tracks
How fragile the psyche
all-seeing in its perceptions
remains invisible
to its own self

At every station
I wait for that one train
Never this one   always the next
I wait at the border
I border on the ridiculous
I border on madness

Another train of thought
another wide junction
Flashing windows of reflection
flashes of recognition
crossbones for crossroads
Always   just up ahead
the graves of the beloved for markers

I   a lost soul
    covered in dust
a trail of red ink behind me
revisit old haunts
my weeping wounds
opening and closing
landscape of regret
memories like smoke in the distance

Every day
I look for that Mirror
the one with a memory
to find my true reflection
Every night
I cross myself   and pray
I make it to the other side

Who am I really?  I ask
Where am I going
and how will I get there?!
I   ALL map with no direction—
    (my broken heart for a compass)
am suspended in that space

between two worlds

I  a Glass Nobody
   country without a name
must
    with the fingertips of the blind
trace my own face   in the dark

## Glass Slipper

*(for my brother, Alexander)*
*To whom much is given, much is expected.*

I know the Prince you speak of
the borrowed magic I must return

How many times have I set my heart for midnight
only to fade into morning?

How many times have I climbed the staircase
that has followed me since childhood?

Nothing is as it seems
Nothing is. As it seems.

In this dream within a Dream
who can tell me what is real and what is not?

The eyes of His Eyes are opening
and I am gathering them like flowers

In this dream within a Dream
who can tell me if I am or if I'm not—

pressed like a petal between Heaven and Earth—
stepping through myself…into another life

**What's Left Unsaid**

Thank you to whomever
belted out "I Did It My Way" in Hungarian
after dragging a dead body
up all one hundred seventeen stairs at five a.m.
Thank you for the light
I might have missed
slowly spilling into my room
Thank you for my room
for whoever turned on the sun
for this fresh almost clean towel
for the kettle that sings good morning
the gracious teacup that holds my coffee

I toast the plant on my windowsill
and pour us both a glass of water
A fine green something or other
with a brand-new leaf
I think I'll call him Buddy
I pat the walls for all the laughter
that never made it past my lips

The television watches over me—
one pale gray eye a little sunken in
He's old and mute now
Hasn't said a word in nearly five years
but I keep him round just the same:
He can't hear me either
as I beat my head against the wall

Thank you for my head by the way
I imagined having a brain tumor
so this blinding migraine comes as such a relief
Thank you
for all that I've been spared—
the terrorist attacks in Paris
the Russian plane crash over Egypt

the earthquake in Nepal
the racial unrest in the States
the plight of the Syrian refugees
the suffering of the homeless hungry
shuffling drooling uncared-for flesh
breathing barely under my own nose

Thank you for my nose
for all these wondrous gifts
e e cummings wrote about in his poem
"thank You God for most this amazing day"
thank you for e e
for smelling touching tasting hearing seeing
though i may forget to thank you for smelling
when I pass through the metro at Châtelet
and other forgotten corners
of leftover urine and lost decay

Thank you
for all the common and uncommon sense
thank you for the nonsense
for loved ones and other strangers who I hold dear
for all those who have sacrificed for us—
some of the great ones
we've never heard their names

Mostly thank you for this day
for the sigh of spirit which moves this breath
for the bruised bones I must polish
before my voyage into the Unknown
for the unnameable angels who hold up the sky
the sparrows who sway on branches I cannot see
for all the things left unsaid
the words yet unspoken

Thank you for the invisible self
who kneels on this page before me

# Acknowledgements

**With gratitude to the following publications in which these poems have appeared:**
*Atlanta Review, Atunis Galaktika Anthology, Beltway Poetry Quarterly, Big Bridge, Counterpunch, Criterion International, Kismet: A Danse Macabre Anthology, Hauptfriedhof: A Danse Macabre Anthology, Facing Feminism,* Ferrandina Press, *Fasihi Magazine, Howl San Francisco Poetry News, Ink Sweat and Tears, Iodine Poetry Journal, Jazz & Literature Anthology, Knot Magazine, Levure Littéraire, Live Encounters, Lothlorien Poetry Journal, Love Love Magazine, Maintenant: Journal of Contemporary Dada Writing and Art, New Generation Beats 2023 Anthology, Occupy Wall Street Anthology, 100 Subtexts, Paris Lit Up Journal, Paris Lit Up: Unbound* (for Printemps des Poètes 2023), *Paris Poets,* Tsunami bOOKS, *Poetica Galactica, Ragged Lion Journal: ERRorISM, Strangers in Paris: New Writing Inspired by the City of Light, The Bastille, The BeZine, The Creative Process, The Opiate, The Original Van Gogh's Ear Anthology, The 7th Quarry, The World Literature Blog, Those That This, Time of the Poet Republic, XXI Century World Literature Anthology, Vox Populi, DoveTales, Writing in a Woman's Voice*

**With love and heartfelt thanks to my patron angels:**
Maximilian Scheuer and Thomas Jeanson

**And other dear friends who have sustained me:**
Alexa Rutherford, Tim Holm, David Barnes, Bruno Charenton, Nina Zivancevic, Matt Jones, Malik Crumpler, Mark Norman Harris, Kara Messenger Jewell, Jason Stoneking, Leslie McAllister, Chris Burke, Carey Downer, Jack Cooper, Bruce Edward Sherfield, Françoise Marbleu, Jill Danger, Ciara Arnette, Birgit Solvsten D'Alpoim Guedes, Linda Maione, Charlie Mercier, Jean Lepegue and James Gebler

## About the Author

Antonia Alexandra Klimenko was first introduced on the BBC and to the literary world by the legendary Meary James Tambimuttu of Editions Poetry London, publisher of T. S. Eliot, Dylan Thomas, Henry Miller and Bob Dylan, to name a few. It was his friend, the late great Kathleen Raine, who took an interest in her writing and encouraged her to publish. A nominee for the Pushcart Prize, The Best of the Net and a former San Francisco Poetry Slam Champion, she is widely published. Her work has appeared in (among others) *XXI Century World Literature* (which she represents France), *The Opiate* and *Maintenant: A Journal of Contemporary Dada Writing and Art*. She is the recipient of the 2018 Generosity Award, bestowed by Kathleen Spivack and Joseph Murray for her outstanding service to international writers through Spoken Word Paris, where she is a writer-in-residence.

www.ingramcontent.com/pod-product-compliance
Lightning Source LLC
LaVergne TN
LVHW032013070526
838202LV00059B/6435